WHEN SUNDIATA KEITA BUILT THE MALI EMPIRE

Ancient History Illustrated Grade 4
Children's Ancient History

BABY PROFESSOR
EDUCATION KIDS

Speedy Publishing LLC

40 E. Main St. #1156

Newark, DE 19711

www.speedypublishing.com

Copyright 2017

In this book, we're going to talk about the life of the Lion King--Sundiata Keita. So, let's get right to it!

WHO WAS SUNDIATA KEITA?

Sundiata Keita was a great ruler and the leader of the Empire of Mali, which was located in Western Africa. His reign lasted twenty years beginning in 1235 AD and ending in 1255 AD. While he was ruler, the Empire of Mali was the most important kingdom in that area.

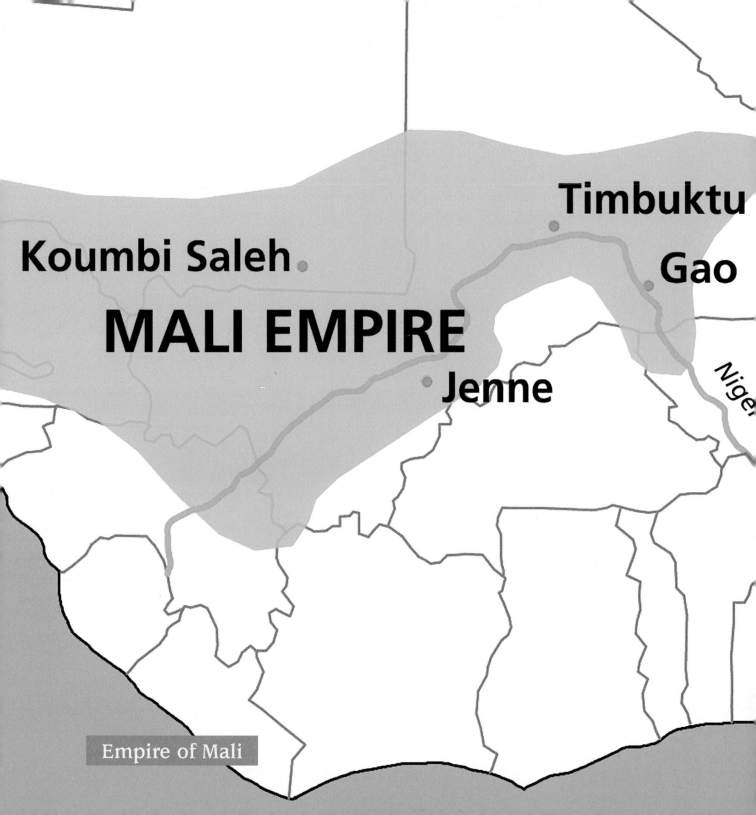

Koumbi Saleh

Timbuktu

Gao

MALI EMPIRE

Jenne

Niger

Empire of Mali

Ghana Mosque

At the beginning of his days as a leader, he only ruled a small Mandinka tribe that was living within the Empire of Ghana. As that empire began to lose power, Sundiata saw his chance. He took control over the Ghana Empire and their lands became a part of his feudal empire.

WHERE WAS THE MALI EMPIRE LOCATED?

• •

The Empire of Mali was located from the coastline of Africa, bordering the Atlantic Ocean, inland over 1,000 miles to the cities of Timbuktu and Gao along the Niger River. Today, six different countries are part of what used to be the Mali Kingdom.

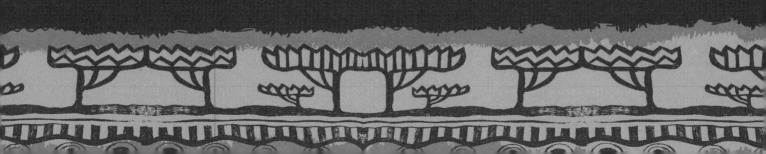

Niger River

Balafoon

THE LEGENDS ABOUT SUNDIATA

When we want to know something about a historical event, we research it in books from the library or sources on the internet. In ancient times, people would tell the stories around a campfire.

Griots

Then, one person would retell the story to another person. The details that we know about Sundiata's early life come from these oral traditions. These tales were told by the

West African griots, who were musicians and storytellers. As the stories were told from one person to another, Sundiata's legend grew.

Muslim Travelers

Eventually, these stories were written down in a book about Sundiata's life called the Sundiata Epic and they also appeared in the manuscripts of some Muslim travelers who wrote about their time in Mali. By the time the oral epic poem about his life was written down, there wasn't a way to verify the facts. As a result, although we know it's a fact that Sundiata founded the Mali Empire, we don't know if every detail from the oral history is true.

SUNDIATA'S MOTHER THE BUFFALO WOMAN

· ·

Sundiata's father was a chief who was named Maghan Kon Fatta, which translated means Maghan the Handsome. The lands he ruled were in the northwest part of the modern country of Guinea.

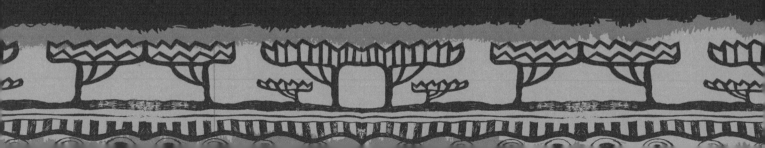

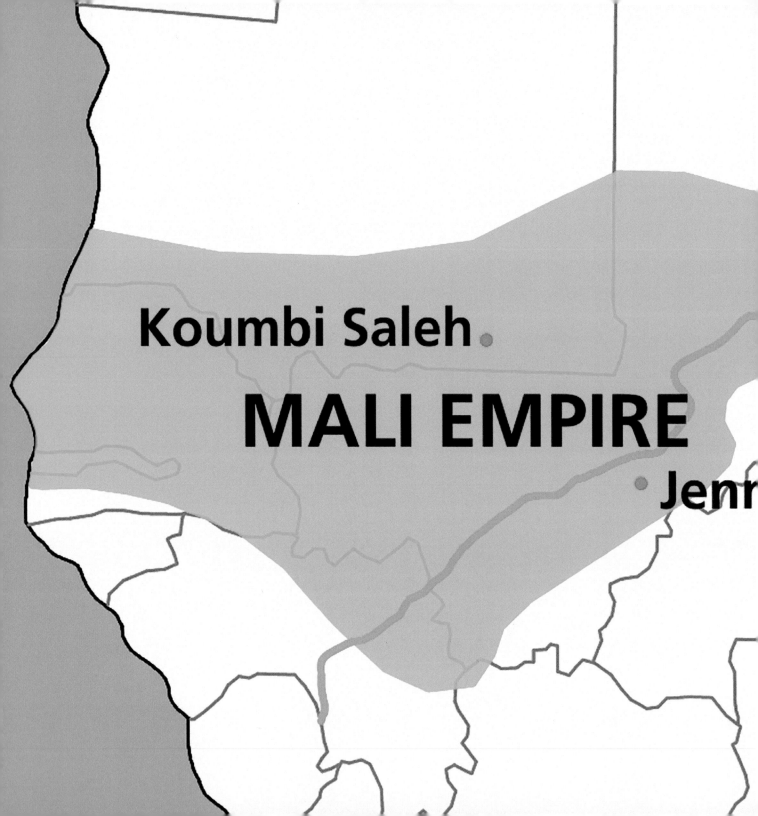

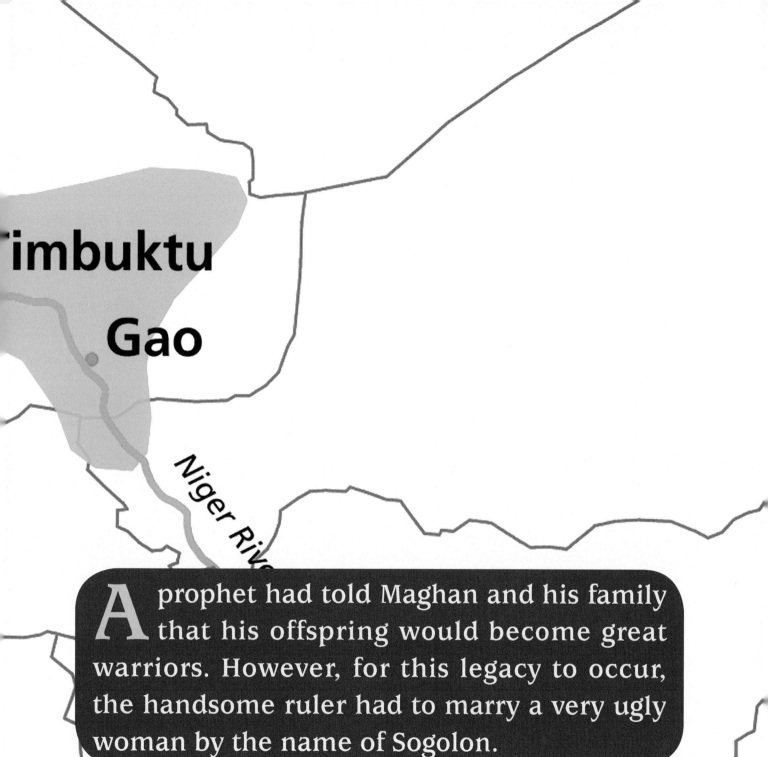

Timbuktu

Gao

Niger Riv

A prophet had told Maghan and his family that his offspring would become great warriors. However, for this legacy to occur, the handsome ruler had to marry a very ugly woman by the name of Sogolon.

One day, two young hunters came to Maghan's court. With them was Sogolon Kedjou. She was engaged to one of the hunters, but when Maghan saw her and confirmed her name, he decided to take her as his second wife. In the epic poem about Sundiata's life, Sogolon is described as hideous to behold. She had eyes that looked pasted on her face and a huge hump that resembled a buffalo's hump on her back.

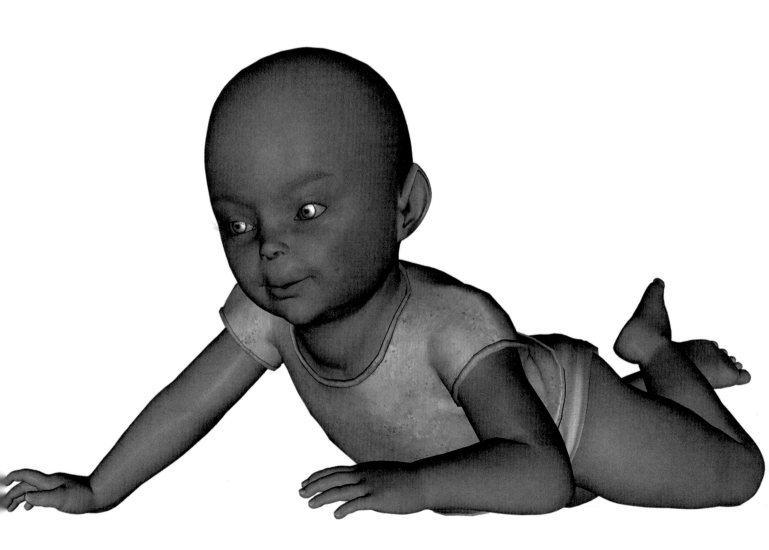

SUDIATA'S EARLY LIFE

Sogolon became pregnant with King Maghan's son, Sundiata, who was born around 1217 AD. Sundiata's parents were dismayed that Sundiata seemed to inherit his mother's qualities instead of his father's. He had a head that seemed huge for his body and large, strange-looking eyes. He was still crawling when other children his age were already walking.

While he was growing up, Sundiata was constantly teased and ridiculed because he was disabled and couldn't walk. However, his father King Maghan still loved him and protected him. King Maghan's first wife, who was called Sassouma, was very upset about this, because she wanted her son to be the king's favorite. Her son's name was Dankaran Touman and she wanted him to inherit the throne.

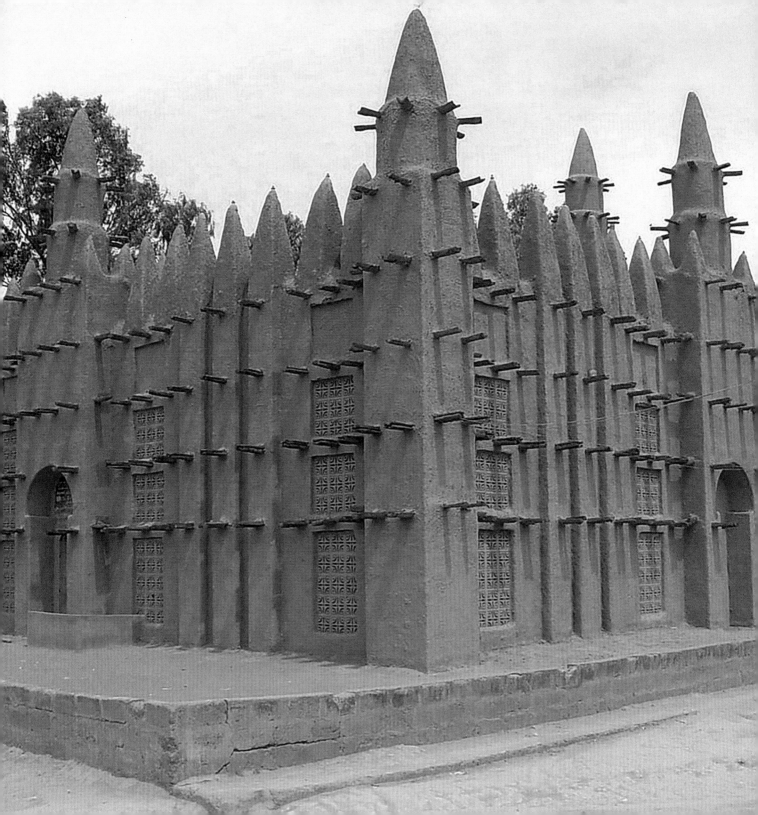

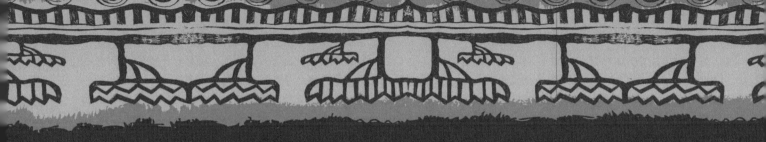

When Sundiata was seven years of age, his father died and the power base shifted. Dankaran Touman became king and Sassouma had gotten what she wanted. Not only that, but a council convened and because Touman was still young they gave Sassouma a great deal of power. She took her revenge out on Sundiata and his mother.

Mosque in Sankore

Now that there was no one to protect them, Sundiata became strong. Through his own work and willpower he learned to improve his body and he was soon able to walk. By the

time he was ten years old, he had transformed from a weak cripple into a young man who had the strength of a lion and who spoke with authority.

Place de Sogolon

SUNDIATA COMES OF AGE

N ow that Sassouma held all the power, Sogolon began to fear for her life and the lives of her children. She was afraid they would be killed. She and her children fled and eventually came to the kingdom of Mema. The king there, who was called Moussa Tounkara, offered to give them protection.

Sundiata became Moussa's favorite, because he had worked so hard to overcome his physical weaknesses and life hardships. Sundiata became an important member of Moussa's court and was eventually appointed viceroy. In this position, he ruled the kingdom while the king was away.

Terracotta Archer figure from Mali

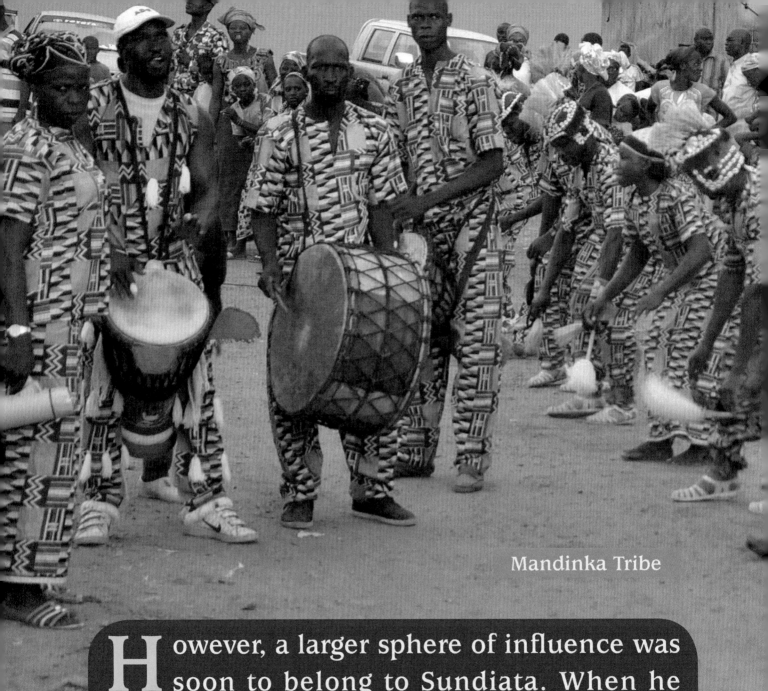

Mandinka Tribe

However, a larger sphere of influence was soon to belong to Sundiata. When he returned to his homeland, the Mandinka had been conquered by the king of Sosso, who was

named Soumaoro Kante. The kingdom of Sosso was treating the Mandinka tribe unfairly and crippling them with taxes.

The people were on the edge of a revolution, but they needed leadership. With the help of a large number of soldiers from Moussa's army, Sundiata went to war against Kante. He had to get many tribes to band together to make this battle successful.

Mali Tribe

Niger River

THE BATTLE OF KIRINA

During the Battle of Kirina, Sundiata shot the Sosso's king with an arrow that had been poisoned. Kante died and it was the first important victory battle that had been led by Sundiata. The battle took place about 1230 AD and marked the beginning of the Mali Empire.

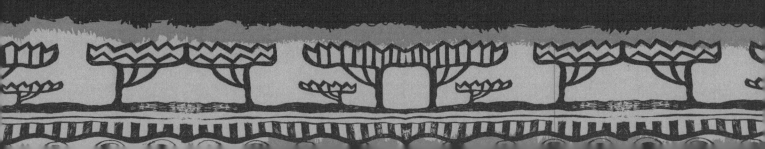

SUNDIATA BECOMES EMPEROR

A fter the Battle of Kirina, Sundiata quickly seized power. He led his soldiers to the Sosso kingdom and conquered them. He also took over the Ghana Empire. He began to establish the Mali Empire and as he did so, he took over the profitable salt and gold trade.

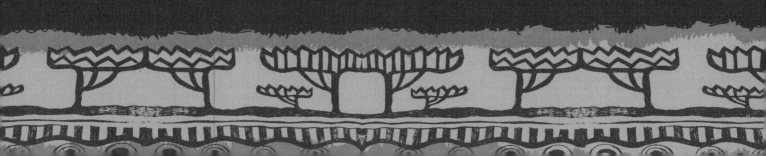

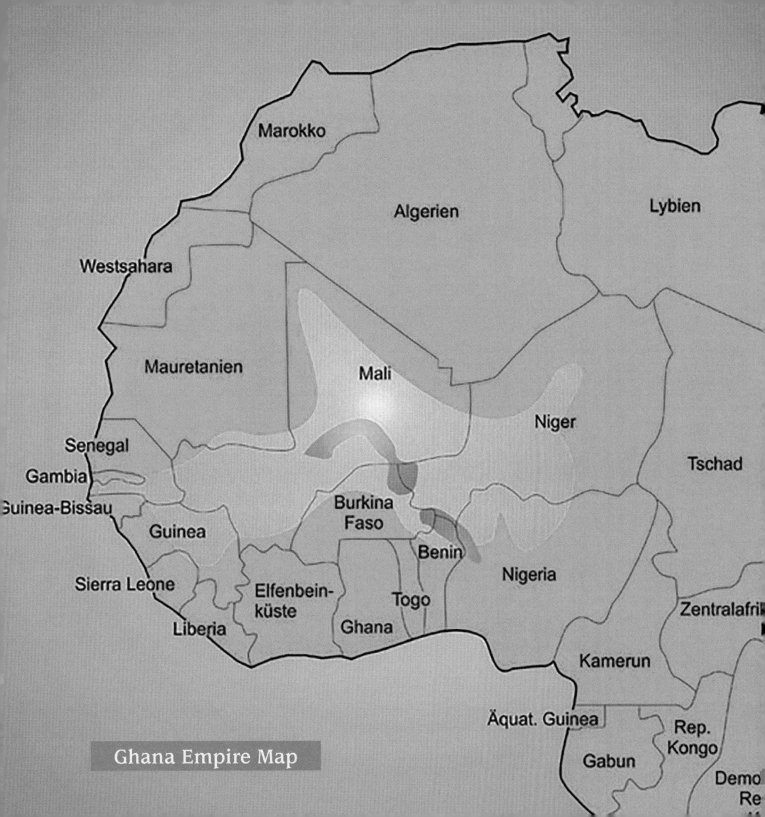

Ghana Empire Map

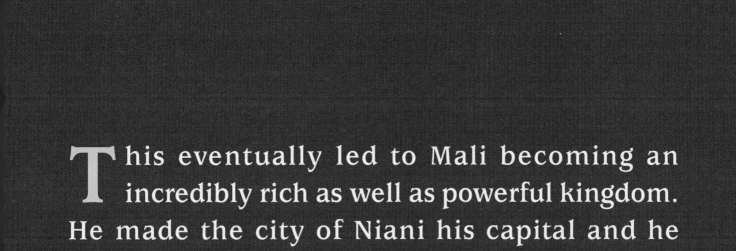

This eventually led to Mali becoming an incredibly rich as well as powerful kingdom. He made the city of Niani his capital and he reigned there for twenty years bringing peace and prosperity to the region.

SUNDIATA'S DEATH

F or the next few centuries, the Mali Empire was the most important kingdom in West Africa. There are different stories regarding Sundiata's death.

Mosque & Place of Assembly at Dramanet Galam

THE LION KING
MINSKOFF THEATRE
DISNEY PRESENTS
THE LION KING
MINSKOFF THEAT

Some say he died when he was drowned in a river and others say that he was killed by a stray arrow during a festival. Mansa Wali who was his son took over the throne upon his death. The legends of Sundiata are still told worldwide today. His story was the inspiration for the popular Disney film called The Lion King.

THE LEGEND OF THE SOSSO BALA

A bala or balafon is a West African musical instrument something like a xylophone. There's a legend that tells that Soumaoro Kante had a magical bala.

It helped him to tell the future, which gave him an advantage in winning battles. He kept the bala to himself. No one else was allowed to touch it. One day, Sundiata's griot, a musician by the name of Balafaseke Kouyate snuck into Kante's court and began playing it.

Balafon

Balafon Players

Kante felt that something was wrong so he went to check on the bala. Caught in the act, Kouyate improvised and sang a song in honor of Kante. Instead of punishing him, Kante hired him. However, Kante had no idea that Kouyate's loyalties were somewhere else. He was loyal to Sundiata Keita and told him the secrets of the Sosso Bala.

The Sosso Bala became a symbol of unity and freedom when Sundiata Keita took power. The Kouyate family has preserved the

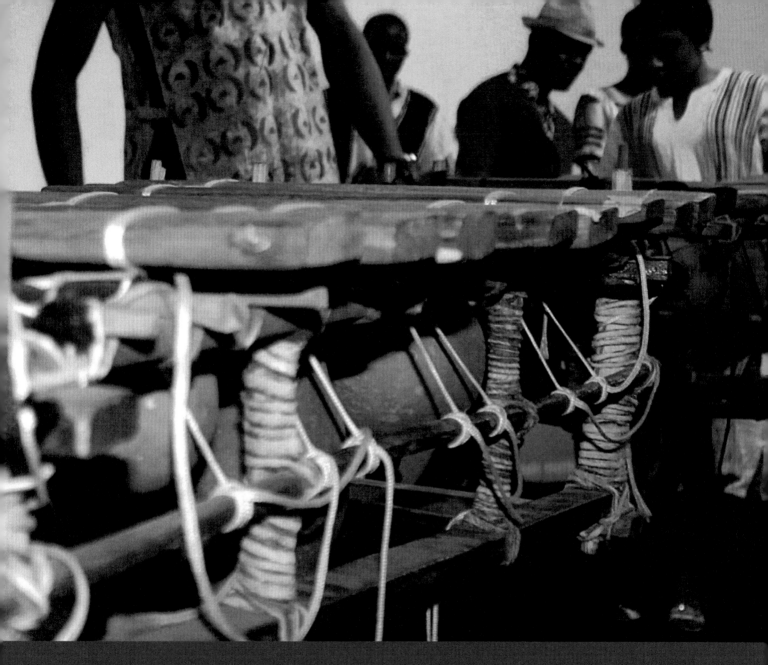

original Sosso Bala. This instrument, now over 800 years old, reminds the people of the glorious past of the Mali Empire.

FASCINATING FACTS ABOUT SUNDIATA KEITA

- He was nicknamed the "Lion King," because he had the strength and bravery of a lion.

- Evidently, Sundiata had the appetite of a lion as well as its strength. He was known for giving sumptuous feasts at his court with huge amounts of food.

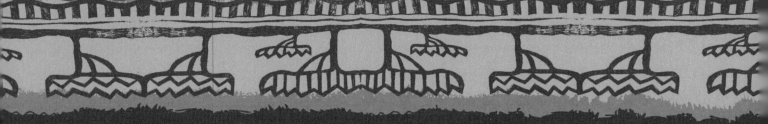

- He was the first king to be awarded the title "Mansa," which translates to the "king of all kings."

- He was a convert to the religion of Islam. However, he didn't force the people in his kingdom to convert.

Islam, Mosque

● He was a wise ruler and divided his kingdom into different parcels. These regions had their own governments and the leaders reported to him.

Gold Mine

- Sundiata's grandnephew became king of Mali in 1312 AD. Due to the gold mines in Mali, he became the richest man in the world. In today's dollars, his fortune may have been worth close to 400 billion.

Awesome! Now you know more about Sundiata Keita and how he built the Mali Empire. You can find more Ancient History books from Baby Professor by searching the website of your favorite book retailer.

Visit

BABY PROFESSOR
EDUCATION KIDS

www.BabyProfessorBooks.com

to download Free Baby Professor eBooks
and view our catalog of new and exciting
Children's Books

87294401R00038

Made in the USA
Lexington, KY
22 April 2018